THE SACRED SYMPATHY OF SORROW.

THE DISCOURSE COMMEMORATIVE OF THE REV. WILLIAM CROSWELL, D.D.

PREACHED IN THE

CHURCH OF THE ADVENT, BOSTON,

(OF WHICH HE WAS RECTOR,)

ON SUNDAY, DECEMBER 7, 1851,

AT THE REQUEST OF THE WARDENS AND VESTRY.

BY THE

RIGHT REV. GEORGE WASHINGTON DOANE, D.D. LL.D.

BISHOP OF NEW JERSEY.

Printed by Request.

BOSTON:

CHARLES STIMPSON,

106, WASHINGTON STREET.

1852.

DE GULIELMO MEO, MORTUO, SUSPIRIUM.

"Ah, my brother!"

ALAS! HOW LIFE DIVIDES ITSELF,
THE LEFT AND THE DEPARTED;
LIKE FUNERAL FILES, IN DOUBLE ROW,
THE DEAD, THE BROKEN-HEARTED!

BOSTON:
WILLIAM CHADWICK, PRINTER,
EXCHANGE STREET.

WILLIAM CROSWELL:

POET, PASTOR, PRIEST;

ENTERED INTO LIFE, SUNDAY, 9 NOVEMBER, (TWENTY-FIRST AFTER TRINITY,) MDCCCLI.

I DID not think to number thee, my Croswell, with the dead,*
But counted on thy loving lips to soothe my dying bed,
To watch the fluttering flood of life ebb languidly away,
And point my spirit to the gate that opens into day.

My "more than brother" thou hast been for five and twenty years,
In storm and shine, in grief and joy, alike in smiles and tears;
Our twin-born hearts so perfectly incorporate in one,
That not the shadow of a thought e'er marred their unison.

Beside me, in life's highest noon, to hear the bridegroom's voice
Thy loving nature fondly stood, contented to rejoice;
Nor boon, that ever bounteous heaven bestowed on me or mine,
But bore, for thee, a keener joy than if it had been thine.

Thy fingers, at the sacred font, when God my hearth had blessed,
Upon my first-born's brow the dear baptismal rite impressed;
My second-born, thine own in Christ, our loving names to blend,
And knit for life his father's son in with his father's friend.

And when our patriarchal WHITE, with Apostolic hands,
Committed to my trembling trust the Saviour's dread commands,
Thy manly form† and saintly face were at my side again,
Thy voice, a trumpet to my heart, in its sincere AMEN.

The Friday before was his forty-seventh birthday.

† "In person, Dr. Croswell was a very pattern of manly beauty."—*Boston Ev. Traveller.*

Beside thee once again be mine, accepted Priest, to stand
And take with thee the pastoral palm from that dear Shepherd's hand.
As thou hast followed Him, be mine in love to follow thee,
Nor care how soon my course be run, so thine my rest may be.

Oh! beautiful and glorious death, with all thy armor on;‡
While, Stephen-like, thy placid face out, like an angel's, shone.§
The words of blessing‖ on thy lips had scarcely ceased to sound,
Before thy gentle soul with them its resting-place had found.

Oh! pastoral and priestly death, poetic as thy life,—
A little child to shelter in Christ's fold from sin and strife,¶
Then, by the gate that opens through the Cross for such as she,**
To enter in thyself, with Christ forevermore to be!

G. W. D.

Riverside, 10th November, 1851.

‡ The Epistle for the Day contained St. Paul's graphic description of "the whole armor of God." His last words, in giving out the hymn, were:

"Soldiers of Christ, arise
And put your armor on."

§ "He never looked so heavenly. His smile upon the infant was ineffable in sweetness." —*MS Letter*,

‖ Unable to rise, after the closing Collect, he said the Benediction on his knees. He died in two hours. A blood-vessel was ruptured in his brain.

¶ He had just baptized an infant; and his sermon was addressed to children.

** "Suffer little children to come unto me, and forbid them not; for *of such is the kingdom of Heaven.*"

DISCOURSE.

How sacred is the sympathy of sorrow! It is the "touch of nature" which "makes the whole world kin." It melted the humanity of Jesus, as He stood by that new grave; and it is with Him, now, that He has "passed into the heavens," and stands where Stephen saw Him, "a great High Priest," "touched with the feeling of our infirmities."

The river which, at first, went out of Eden is salt and bitter since the Fall. It is the river, now, of tears, and waters still the world which man inhabits. The electric spark which, in twelve hours, had flashed your sorrow on my heart, opened its secret sources and overflowed my manhood. I have wept among my children; I have wept beside his grave; and I am here to weep with you.

It was an ancient Roman superstition that the place was sacred which the lightning struck. How sacred must the spot be ever held where I now stand, on which the lambent flame of love from God did but dissolve the bonds which held it here, to set the spirit of our darling free, and bid it welcome to the heaven which Christ had opened for it! And how cold and dead must be our hearts, if, in the light of such an Euthanasia, they be not waked from their dull dreams of earth, and do not imp their wings to take the upward flight by which he went to be with Jesus! Oh, that the simple words which I am now (please God,) to speak, may have, through grace, the unction of his life; may bear, through grace, the urgent warning of his death; may win your souls, through grace, to holiness, with the attraction which drew him to Heaven!

William Croswell was born in Hudson, New York, on the 7th day of November, 1804. He was among that great company of the preachers who were not born in the Church which their hearts have afterwards embraced, and to which their lives have been devoted. He was thus not baptized till 1813, before which time his father had removed to Albany, and had become a Churchman. A nobler Churchman does not live, nor one that has done better service to the Church, than the Rector of Trinity Church, New Haven. The lines which William has recorded with the date of his own two-and-thirtieth birthday, need no deduction on the score of filial love, but are as true as if they were not written by a son.

"My father, proud am I to bear
  Thy face, thy form, thy stature;
But happier far, might I but share
  More of thy better nature;
Thy patient progress after good,
  All obstacles disdaining;
Thy courage, faith, and fortitude,
  And spirit uncomplaining.

"Then, for the day that I was born
Well might I joy, and borrow
No longer of the coming morn
Its trouble or its sorrow:
Content I'd be to take my chance
In either world, possessing,
For my complete inheritance,
Thy virtues and thy blessing."

It is not now the time to dwell upon his childhood or his youth. He was, throughout, a loving and obedient son, singularly true and just in thought and word and deed, transparent in his conscientiousness as purest chrystal. As an instance of it: when a child at school, he was called up by his master, and sharply reproved for talking. "No, sir," his answer was, "I was not talking; but I was just going to!" The boy was "father of the man." He was devout from his childhood, and had read the Bible so constantly that most of it was in his memory. The memories of home have never found a fitter utterance than in the lines,—worthy of Burns and like him,—which he addressed to his when he had left it for the world.

"I knew my father's chimney-top,
Though nearer to my heart than eye;
And watched the blue smoke reeking up
Between me and the winter sky.

"Wayworn, I traced the homeward track
My wayward youth had left with joy;
Unchanged in soul I wandered back,
A man in years, in heart a boy.

"I thought upon its cheerful hearth,
And cheerful hearts' untainted glee;
And felt, of all I'd seen on earth,
This was the dearest spot to me."

And seldom has a pious mother's influence been owned more feelingly and faithfully than in the lines addressed to his, when he was thirty years of age:

"Oft, as I muse on all the wrong,
  The silent grief, the secret pain,
My froward youth hath caused, I long
  To live my childhood o'er again.
And yet they are not all in vain,
  The lessons which thy love then taught;
Nor always has it dormant lain,
  The fire from thy example caught.

"And now, as feelings all divine
  With deepest power my spirit touch,
I feel as if some prayer of thine,
  My mother! were availing much.
Thus be it ever more and more,
  Till it be thine in bliss to see
The hopes, with which thy heart runs o'er
  In fondest hours, fulfilled in me."

We are reminded of Saint Augustine's mother by these lines, and feel the assurance which was given to her, that the child of prayers and tears, like hers, could not be lost. His early education was received in New Haven* and its neighborhood. He was, at one period, the Catechumen of him whom the whole Church rejoices in as Bishop of Western New York, Doctor Delancey, then a student in Yale College; and he never ceased to speak of his instructions with the most affectionate and grateful reverence. He

* He was prepared for college by an excellent teacher, Mr. Joel Jones, since greatly distinguished as Mayor of the city of Philadelphia, a Judge in its highest Courts, and President of Girard College.

was himself, also, a graduate of the same ancient and distinguished University, having received the degree of Bachelor of Arts in 1822. His first Communion was at the Christmas in that year. He did not become a Candidate for Orders till 1826. Though evidently destined for the ministry, his diffidence and self-distrust kept him back. For a while, he contemplated the practice of medicine as his profession. His theological studies were pursued, in part, at the General Seminary, but chiefly under the direction of the excellent Bishop of Connecticut, whom, now my brother, it is *my* pleasure also to acknowledge as my Master in theology. It was in 1826 that our intimate relations commenced; and man has never been in closer bonds with man, than he with me, for five-and-twenty years. A letter from him to a mutual friend, the witness and the sharer of our earliest years of happiness, brings down the tokens of his unreserving confidence and perfect love within the latest fortnight of his life. I do not hesitate to speak thus personally, because your invitation to me, to preach here, is predicated mainly on these intimate relations; and, only for their dear sake, could I have left my duties to be with you.

He came to Hartford when I was then Professor in Washington (now Trinity) College, at Bishop Brownell's instance, to be associated with me in the direction of the Episcopal Watchman. I remember, as if it were but yesterday, our earliest meeting at a hearth as bright and blessed* as was ever kindled

* When I name Dr. Sumner's, how many hearts will answer! She, who was its chiefest joy, was taken from her loved ones with as little warning as our dear mutual friend. "How grows, in Paradise, our store!"

by the glow of Christian hospitality; and never was a happier circle gathered than met there, almost nightly, for years. Our intercourse was intimate at once, and we never had a feeling or a thought to part us. His contributions to the Watchman were chiefly poetical. The following sonnet was the first.

"Oh, THOU, whom slumber reacheth not nor sleep,
The Guardian God of Zion, in whose sight
A thousand years pass like a watch at night,
Her battlements and high munitions keep,
Or else the WATCHMAN waketh but in vain!
Him, in his station newly set, make strong,
And, in his vigils, vigilant; sustain
His overwearied spirit in its long
And lonely round, from eve till matin song;
And of Thy charge remind him,—'WATCH AND PRAY!'
So, whether coming at the midnight bell,
Or at cockcrowing, or at break of day,
Thou find him faithful, and say—'All is well!'
'How rich is the reward of that true Sentinel!'

Could it have been any better, or any different, if he had been premonished of his course through life, or if he had written it on the day on which his life was closed? His poetical contributions to the Episcopal Watchman were numerous, in addition to his invaluable services as editor; and they won for him a high and honorable place among the very few to whom the name of Poet can be given. Everything that he ever wrote in verse was strictly occasional. It was so much of his heart-life set to music. He lived it, every line. And it was all inspired at the hearth-side, or at the altar-foot. It was domestic often, always sacred.

He fulfilled, in every verse, that beautiful suggestion of the sky-lark to the mind of Wordsworth,—

> "Type of the wise, who soar but never roam,
> True to the kindred points of heaven and home."

In that incomparable modesty, which set off, in its mild opal light, his virtues and his graces, he thought very poorly of these admirable productions, and has half suggested the desire that they remain still fugitive. But this must not be suffered. They are part and parcel of his nature, and of his office. As he lived them, so he preaches in them, and will while the Gospel shall be preached. What could more clearly vindicate for him the name of Christian Poet, than his lines, entitled "The Ordinal," written on the day of his ordination by Bishop Brownell, in his father's church, at New Haven, Saint Paul's day, 1829.

> "Alas for me if I forget
> The memory of that day
> Which fills my waking thoughts, nor yet
> E'en sleep can take away!
> In dreams I still renew the rites,
> Whose strong but mystic chain
> The spirit to its God unites,
> And none can part again.
>
> How oft the Bishop's form I see,
> And hear that thrilling tone
> Demanding with authority
> The heart for God alone.
> Again I kneel as then I knelt,
> While he above me stands,
> And seem to feel as then I felt
> The pressure of his hands.

Again the priests in meet array,
As my weak spirit fails,
Beside me bend them down to pray
Before the chancel rails ;
As then, the Sacramental host
Of God's elect are by,
When many a voice its utterance lost,
And tears dimmed many an eye.

As then they on my vision rose,
The vaulted aisles I see,
And desk and cushioned book repose
In solemn sanctity,—
The mitre o'er the marble niche,
The broken crook and key
That, from a Bishop's tomb, shone rich
With polished tracery.

The hangings, the baptismal font,
All, all, save me, unchanged,
The holy table, as was wont,
With decency arranged ;
The linen cloth, the plate, the cup,
Beneath their covering shine,
Ere priestly hands are lifted up
To bless the bread and wine.

The solemn ceremonial past,
And I am set apart
To serve the Lord, from first to last,
With undivided heart ;
And I have sworn, with pledges dire
Which God and man have heard,
To speak the holy truth entire
In action and in word.

Oh Thou ! who, in Thy holy place,
Hast set Thine orders three,
Grant me, Thy meanest servant, grace
To win a good degree :

That so replenished from above,
And in my office tried,
Thou mayst be honoured, and in love
Thy Church be edified!"

I had come to Boston in 1828, and in 1829 he came here,* to Christ Church, as successor to the Rev. Dr. Eaton; who, spared in providential love to wend his patriarchal way among the children's children of his first parishioners, was strangely called to commend the parting spirit of his son and brother in the faith and ministry of Christ, into the hands of Him who gave it. He was ordained a Priest, and instituted Rector of Christ Church, on Saint John Baptist's Day, 1829, by the venerable Bishop Griswold. How he loved the very dust that generations had gathered upon that ancient edifice; how faithfully he did his Master's work there, for eleven years; how much he attached to him the affectionate confidence of his parishioners; how many feet he gathered within the fold; how many souls he knit into the faith of Jesus Christ, there are those here, who know and can bear witness. How deeply his heart yearned to leave its time honored walls, when called to another scene of pastoral labor,† his

* A mutual friend, who knew him thoroughly and loved him even more, reminds me that my first remark after being established here, was, "*Now, we must have Croswell!*" On his first appearance in Christ Church, another of the three who were to me as Noah, Daniel, and Job, said to him, "*How do you like Mr. Doane's friend?* "*Oh*," was his prompt reply, "*he looks as amiable as Dr. Watts!*"

† He took with him, to the Diocese of Western New York, the following dismissory letter:

Dear Sir: The object of this, is to transfer from the State of Massachusetts to your Diocese, the Rev. William Croswell. Merely to say, that, for three

loving spirit has borne testimony in one of his own most beautiful and touching lyrics. How warmly he had cherished, and how faithfully he had kept alive the feeling of his ordination, another of them, bearing date at noon, on the sixth anniversary of that event, and apparently written while alone, within its hallowed walls, most fervently declares.

"How swift the years have come and gone, since on this blessed day,
A victim at the altar's horn, I gave myself away;
And, streaming through the House of God, a glory seemed to shine,
Invisible to other eyes, but manifest to mine.

* * * * * *

Oh! father, mother, brethren, 'friends, no less than brethren dear,'
Who promised, at this solemn hour to be in spirit near,
Say, is it not your influence in blended prayer I feel,
As now, before the Mercy-seat, from many shrines we kneel!

I would my heart might ever thus dissolve with fervent heat,
As here, 'fast by the oracle,' the service I repeat,
That ever, in my inmost soul, the same rejoicing light
Might burn, like Zion's altar flame, unquenchable and bright."

Four years he ministered as Rector of Saint Peter's Church, Auburn, earnestly, faithfully, most acceptably, and most successfully. But Boston had been the scene of the labors of his earliest love. His tastes

years last past he has not been justly liable to evil report, for error in doctrine, or viciousness of life, though eminently true, seems, in his case, very unnecessary. He will leave behind him no clergyman more highly, more justly, or more generally esteemed, for those qualities which constitute and adorn the gentleman, the scholar, and the faithful minister of Christ. While, with many hundreds of others, I deeply regret his loss to this Diocese, I may well congratulate you on such an accession to yours. That, in his new situation, he may find friends as numerous and as cordial as those he leaves, is the prayer of your friend and brother, A. V. GRISWOLD.

To the Right Rev. Dr. DeLancey."

and habits inclined him to a city life. The bonds of nature drew this way. And more than all, his heart was yearning to dissolve itself upon a ministry among the poor. It was no recent passion. It was the sacred fancy of his youth. Hours and hours had we discoursed of it together. His labors, while connected with Christ Church, had partaken largely of that character. He had been every body's minister, that had no other. He had qualified himself to be the servant of Christ's poor; and, in his yearning nature, he could brook no other service. What could be plainer proof of this than the following lines, which he wrote in 1830, and which, ten days before his death, he copied out and sent to a Church paper, in New York, in which the claims of the poor find a devoted advocate!

"Lord! lead the way the Saviour went,
By lane and cell obscure,
And let love's treasures still be spent
Like His, upon the poor.

Like Him, through scenes of deep distress
Who bore the world's sad weight,
We in their crowded loneliness
Would seek the desolate.

For Thou hast placed us side by side
In this wide world of ill;
And, that Thy followers may be tried,
The poor are with us still.

Mean are all offerings we can make;
But Thou hast taught us, Lord,
If given for the Saviour's sake,
They lose not their reward."

Who could have any doubt as to where *his* heart was, who wrote these verses one-and-twenty years ago? Who but admires the stedfastness of purpose and unrelenting self-devotion to a sacred cause, which, after one-and-twenty years, could reproduce, and re-adopt and re-assert them? Who that loves him, or loves his Lord, would have his latest contributions to the service of the Gospel, any other, in line or letter, than this is. Beautifully, feelingly, fervently did he adopt, for the conclusion of the letter which enclosed it,—may we all have grace to do so!—the admirable pre-Advent collect: "Stir up, we beseech thee, O Lord, the wills of Thy faithful people; that they plenteously bringing forth the fruit of good works, may, by Thee, be plenteously rewarded, through Jesus Christ, our Lord."

In 1844, these longings of his pious heart were met. A sufficient number of like-minded persons was found to organize a Church, whose sittings should be free, that all who would, might come; which should be supported, through the channel of the weekly Offertory, that every one might lay up, on the Lord's day, as the Apostle hath enjoined, according to his ability; which should celebrate daily Morning and Evening Prayer, in accordance with the order of the Prayer Book, and so be "a House of Prayer for all people." His first meeting with the Corporation of the Church of the Advent, was on the eve of November 9th, 1844—by a strange coincidence, the very day, whose seventh return was to take their Rector from their head. The worship, for six months, was, as the

easier access to the poor, the ignorant, the vicious, the degraded. He won their confidence, at once. And the more they saw of him, the more they trusted. He was so considerate of their feelings. He was so charitable to their infirmities. He was so constant in his assiduity. He knew the strings in every broken heart; and had, from God, the medicine to heal their hurts. He seemed a ministering angel to them; and they glorified God in him. But, especially, he was so unreserved in his self-sacrifice. One says of him, "Dr. Croswell was instant, in season and out of season. He never was known to refuse any call for service or duty."* And another,† than whom no living man knows better what Christ's servant with the poor should be, speaks thus of him, in words, which coming from the heart go to it. "How they loved him! Because he was like his Master. Of Him he had learned to 'be pitiful, to be courteous' to the poorest, to the humblest. How hard it is to be like him; so true,—so simple in doing good!—The distance was never too great for him to go, to do good, for Christ's sake—the storm was never too severe for him to find his way through it, to relieve a tossed and beaten sufferer—the night was never too late, nor too dark, for him to find his way, to bear the Cross, with its consolations, to the bed of death." How plainly I can see him now; with his old cloak wrapped about him, which he would gladly have given to the next poor man, if he had thought it good enough

* Ms. letter.

† The Rev. E. M. P. Wells, of Saint Stephen's House, Boston, Missionary to the poor, in his last Annual Report of his labors, in the city of Boston.

for him; and with his huge over-shoes, which, when he put them on so deliberately, would always bring to mind what the Apostle said, about having the "feet shod with the preparation of the Gospel of peace." As he set out upon his ministry of mercy you might think him very slow, and doubt if he would find his way, and wonder when he would get back, or if he ever would. But, ere he slept, he would have threaded every darkest and most doleful lane, in the most destitute quarter of the city, dived into cellars, and climbed garrets, comforted a lonely widow, prayed by a dying sailor, administered the Holy Communion to an old bed-ridden woman, carried some bread to a family of half-starved children, engaged a mother to be sure and send her youngest daughter to an infant school, and "made a sunshine," in the shadiest places of human suffering and sorrow. And, when all this was done, if he had time for it, he would charm the most refined and intellectual with his delightful conversation and his pure and lambent playfulness. With a manner that seemed quite too quiet, there was an undercurrent of ceaseless, irrepressible activity; and brightest thoughts, in happiest words, were ever oozing out, like fragrant gums, from some East Indian tree, as soft, as sweet, as balmy, as balsamic. "He was a scholar, and a ripe and good one." I may add, as justly; "exceeding wise, fairspoken, and persuading." He had an intuition for good books, and the best parts of them; as he had also for good men.* With

* One of the keenest knowers I have ever met, observed of him, that his knowledge of men was most remarkable. "It was hard to get his judgment," he remarked; "but when you had it, it was a good one. He was a staff that you might lean on, sure that it would neither bend nor break."

all he did, and with the little that he seemed to do—the very reverse of Chaucer's Sergeant, who "seemed besier than he was;" he was at home in all good English learning with perfect mastery among the poets. His classical attainments were much beyond the average. He was a well read divine; and, beyond any man I knew, was "mighty in the Scriptures" and skilful in his application of them. His sermons were entirely practical. The object of his preaching was apparent always:—to make men better. He sunk himself entirely in his theme:—CHRIST JESUS, AND HIM CRUCIFIED. He had no manner. Yet the perfect conviction which he carried with him from the first, that he was really in earnest, made him attractive to all sorts of people, high and low, rich and poor, wise and simple, ignorant and learned, and made him profitable to all. And, whatever his discourse might be, in matter or in manner, there was the cogent application always, of a holy and consistent life. His habits were simple, almost to severity. "Having food and raiment," he was "therewith content." What remained, after necessities were met, was so much for the poor. He was a Churchman of the noblest pattern. A Churchman of the Bible, and of the Prayer Book. A Churchman, with Andrews, and Taylor, and Wilson. If he was least tolerant of any form of error, it was that of PAPAL ROME. He would have burned, if need had been, with Latimer and Ridley. He made no compromise with novelties, but always said "the old is better." There was no place for the fantastic in *his* churchmanship; it was taken up, too much, with daily work, and daily prayer, and daily caring for the poor. There was no antagonism between his poetry and practice. His poetry was practical. It was the way-flower of his daily life; its violet, its cowslip, or its pansy.* It sprang up where he walked. You could not get a letter from him, though made up of the details of business or the household trifles of his hearth, that some sweet thought, (as natural as it was beautiful,) would not bubble up above the surface with prismatic hues that marked it his. His heart was wholly in the priesthood. He loved to pray. He loved to minister the Sacrament. He loved to preach. He loved to catechize the children. And, when he lifted up his manly voice in the old hymns and anthems of the Church, it seemed as if a strain of the eternal worship had strayed down from heaven. He was so modest and retiring that few knew him well. But there is no one that knew him well, that will not say, with me, "we shall not look upon his like again." If he excelled in any one relation, after his service to Christ's poor, it was in all the acts and offices of friendship. He was a perfect friend. So delicate, so thoughtful, so candid, so loving, so constant. "More than my brother," for a quarter of a century, I dare not trust myself to speak of what he was to me; of what I know I was to him. I never heard words spoken, with sincerer pleasure, than when, the other

* How fond he was of flowers! Beautiful tributes of this kind, went with him into the grave. He was a fond lover of music, too. He not only took a leading part in the music of the Church, but employed his exquisite taste in its selection. So that its whole character was singularly tender, touching, and impressive.

day, his old heroic father—who might well declare, with aged Ormond, that "he would not exchange his dead son, for any living son, in Christendom"—said to the coachman who had driven us out to weep together by his grave,* "*This is the Bishop of New Jersey; the best friend that my son ever had, on earth.*" I would not covet for my child a richer earthly treasure, or a higher human praise, than to be William Croswell's best and dearest friend.

And, "Lycidas is dead; dead, ere his prime!" In the midst of his years and of his usefulness. When a keener enjoyment of his social and domestic comforts had been awakened in him. When the work, which he loved beyond his life, was prosperous to his heart's content. When he was looking out on life, after some years of trial and discouragement, not without physical suffering, with a more cheerful aspect. When the just estimate of his invaluable services had placed his family with him in a convenient mansion, with becoming fixtures; so that he said to one, in his own pleasant way, "my feet are set in a large room." When he had put in order his personal and parochial papers. When he had planned for the Advent season, in which he so delighted, the training of a class for Confirmation, and had begun his course of teaching. When he had met his brethren and old friends at Hartford, at the recent Consecration there; and enjoyed them all, with a peculiar zest. When he had spent a happy day beside his father's hearth; glad that it rained, that he might stay at home and

* His mortal part rests in the burying ground at New Haven. It was his desire, recorded years ago, that he might be buried " deep in the ground."

have them all to his own self: and said that he felt so much better, that he believed he would resume his old poetic trade. When he had spent, with his domestic dear ones, the interval of Sunday, with an even more than wonted cheerfulness; making his latest personal memorandum; and even dating the letter which his little daughter was to send to her grandfather the next day. When he had secured within the fold of Christ the little child of a dear friend, whose baptism had, for weeks, been providentially delayed. When he was yet engaged in the choicest work of his true pastoral heart, in feeding the lambs of Jesus, and had not yet wholly preached the sermon which he had prepared for little children. In an instant, "in the twinkling of an eye," (so that he gave the hymn from memory which he could not find in his familiar prayer-book,* and had to say the benediction on his knees,†) in an instant, "in the twinkling of an eye," "the silver cord" was "loosed, the golden bowl" was "broken, the pitcher" was "broken at the fountain, the wheel" was "broken at the cistern,

* It is remarkable that, in his embarrassment, though he gave out the first line of the eighty-eighth hymn, "Soldiers of Christ, arise!" he announced it by number as the *one hundred* and eighty-eighth, the third verse of which is as follows:—

"Determined are the days that fly
Successive o'er thy head;
The numbered hour is on the wing,
That lays thee with the dead."

In two hours he was "with the dead."

† An admirable sermon by the Lord Bishop of Fredericton, preached in the Church of the Advent, three Sundays before Dr. Croswell's death, contains the following sentence:—"Suppose we were to be seized with a stroke of paralysis, or of any sudden disease, where could we be found with so much comfort as on our knees, in public prayer?" How strange a coincidence!

the dust" returned "to the earth, as it was, and the spirit unto God who gave it." A vein, that had been overtasked in that majestic form, (so beautiful in death that one described it, when it had reached New Haven, as resembling some exquisite master-piece of statuary,*) had yielded to the rushing current of the life-blood from the brain; and there was a widow and an orphan in his house, and sheep without a shepherd in his fold; his aged parents and devoted brothers were bereaved of their darling; the twin was taken from my heart; Christ's "poor had lost a— Croswell."†

Can I conclude in fitter words than in his own, when I had written him, in 1834, of the last hours of my dear friend, the Rev. Dr. Montgomery: "Your last most touching letter has made me weep with them that weep, and left my heart more tender than ever to the sacred sorrows of this week of the Passion. The following lines, the sincere impulse of my feelings, arranged themselves, almost spontaneously, as they stand: —

"My brother, I have read
Of holy men, in Christ who fell asleep,
For whom no bitter tears of woe were shed;
I could not weep.

"And thou thyself art one,
O man of loves, and truth without alloy!
The Master calleth, and thy work well done,
Enter thy joy!

* Every one spoke of his singular beauty in death. He was buried in his customary dress, over which was the surplice. It was one that had belonged to his friend, and mine, the Rev. Edward G. Prescott, who died at sea, on his voyage to Fayal. He has scarcely written anything more beautiful than this tribute to his memory. (See p. 27.)

† The Rev. Mr. Wells' Report.

"To such as thee belong
The harmonies in which all Heaven unite,
To share the 'inexpressive nuptial song'
And walk in white.

"And oh! thy church, thy home,
Thy widowed home! — Who shall forbid to grieve?
How may they bear the desolating gloom
Such partings leave?

"Great Shepherd of the flock!
Even Thou whose life was given for the sheep,
Sustain them in the overwhelming shock,
And safely keep!"

Three words, beloved, and I have done. His "home," his "widowed home," will you leave that uncomforted? His work, his glorious work, will you leave that to falter? His teaching, his example, the beauty of his saintly life, the perfect beauty of his glorious and triumphant death, shall they be lost upon your hearts? Shall they be lost upon your lives?* Oh! for the testimony, if they are, that he will bear against you, when you stand with him before the Judge! Oh! for the blessedness and glory, if you bear the cross of Jesus Christ as he did, and conquer with him in that sign, which shall be yours when you shall enter with him the celestial fold, and be with him for ever with the Lamb!

* Nothing could exceed the solemnity and impressiveness of all the arrangements after his death. Thousands visited the remains, most of them of the poor for whom he lived. The Church was filled with mourners, the Bishop of the Diocese, with the assistant Bishop of Connecticut, and above sixty of the clergy being present. The admirable resolutions of the Wardens and Vestry well express their feelings and the feelings of the Parishioners. (See p. 29.)

Resolutions were also adopted by the Clergy, assembled at the house of the Bishop, he himself presiding, and by the Vestry of Christ Church.

ELEGIAC:

Written in a copy of Milton, presented by the Rev. E. G. Prescott, who died on his passage to the Azores, on the third day after his departure, on the morning of the eleventh of April, 1844.

Thy cherished gift, departed friend,
  With trembling I unfold,
And fondly gaze upon its lids
  In crimson wrought and gold ;
I open to its dirge-like strain
  Of one who died at sea, —
And as I read of Lycidas
  I think, the while, of thee.

Thy languid spirit sought, in vain
  The beautiful Azores,
But ere it reached the middle main,
  Was rapt to happier shores.
As in a dream-like halcyon calm,
  It entered on its rest,
Amid the groves of Paradise,
  And islands of the blest.

Kind friends afar, at thy behest,
  Had fitted bower and hall
To entertain their kindred guest
  In ever-green Fayal ;
In greener bowers thy bed is made,
  And sounder is thy sleep
Than ever life had known, among
  The chambers of the deep.

No mark along the waste may tell
  The place of thy repose,
Yet there is ONE who loved thee well,
  And loved by thee, who knows ;
And though now sunk, like Lycidas,
  Beneath the watery floor,
Yet HIS great might that walked the waves,
  Shall thy dear form restore.

Though years must first pass by, no time
  His purpose shall derange,
And in His guardianship thy soul
  Shall suffer no "sea-change."
And when the depths give back their charge,
  Oh! may our welcome be
With thine, among Christ's ransomed throngs,
  Where there is no more sea!

PARISH OF THE ADVENT, BOSTON:
Sunday, the 22nd after Trinity, A. D. 1851.

At a meeting of the *Wardens and Vestry*, holden at the Church immediately after evening service, the committee appointed to proceed to New Haven in company with the body of the late Rector of this Parish,—the Reverend WILLIAM CROSWELL, D. D.,—and to attend to its interment at that place, *reported*, that they had discharged the duty assigned to them; the body having been buried at 11 o'clock, on the morning of the 13th of November, at the New Haven Cemetery, "*deep in the ground*," in accordance with the wishes of the deceased. The following resolution was thereupon adopted by a unanimous vote, and entered at large upon the record.

Resolved, That now, for the first time, when the last rites have been paid to the mortal remains of our beloved Rector, we will strive for a moment to control our grief, and to give expression, in some feeble degree, to what *no words can measurably express*.

Although it does not become us to sorrow as others which have no hope, yet we cannot behold the desolation of our House of Prayer, and remember the affliction which weighs upon the family of our beloved Rector, without offering to them the testimony of our sympathy and condolence.

We, therefore, the Church and Congregation whom he served, are ready to bear witness concerning our brother, appointed to the Priesthood over us:

That he duly exercised his Ministry to the honor of GOD and the edifying of HIS Church:

That he considered well with himself the end of his Ministry towards the children of GOD, towards the Spouse and Body of Christ:

That he never ceased his labors, his care and diligence, but did all that lay in him to bring all such as were committed to his charge unto an agreement in the FAITH and knowledge of GOD, and to ripeness and perfectness of age in CHRIST:

That he was a faithful dispenser of the Word of GOD, and of HIS Holy Sacraments:

That without preferring one before another, and doing nothing by partiality, he did not shun to declare unto all, high and low, rich and poor, one with another, *the whole counsel of* GOD; warning us that, without exemption or dispensation, we must obey *both the greatest and the very least* of the Holy Commandments of JESUS CHRIST.

And now since we, among whom he had gone preaching the Kingdom of GOD, shall see his face on earth no more, we take record that he is *pure from the blood of all men.*

We remember that by the space of seven years he ceased not to warn every one, morning and evening, with his prayers, taking heed unto himself and to all the Flock over which the HOLY GHOST had made him Overseer, feeding the Church of GOD, which HE hath purchased with HIS own Blood.

And while we sorrow most of all for the words which we *must* speak—"we shall see his face no more,"—we are consoled by the remembrance, that *when his* LORD *came he was found watching;—as one that waiteth for his* LORD;—*his loins girded about with priestly robes, and the spiritual lights of his Ministration burning;*—and we therefore call upon his family to bow with us in humble resignation to the mysterious Will of GOD, and with us to—

BLESS HIS HOLY NAME for all HIS servants departed this life in HIS faith and fear; beseeching HIM to give us Grace so to follow their good examples, that with them we may be partakers of HIS heavenly Kingdom. Grant this, O Father, for JESUS CHRIST, his sake, our only Mediator and Advocate. AMEN!

www.ingramcontent.com/pod-product-compliance
Lightning Source LLC
LaVergne TN
LVHW011136110826
845150LV00008B/2381

* 9 7 8 1 4 1 8 1 9 4 5 3 6 *